STAR WARS®

Who's Who

D1154192

Library of Congress Cataloging-in-Publication Number 97-76142

ISBN 0-7624-0321-7

This book may be ordered by mail from the publisher.
Please include $1.00 for postage and handling.

But try your bookstore first!

Running Press Book Publishers
125 South Twenty-second Street
Philadelphia, Pennsylvania 19103-4399

Introduction

Although the *Star Wars* trilogy featured groundbreaking special effects, George Lucas knew special effects alone would not tell his story. The saga was driven by the characters, the heroes and villains who hoped to change the course of history throughout their galaxy. Focused on Luke Skywalker, a farm boy who dreamed of adventure beyond his desert home on Tatooine, the story appealed to the dreamers in us all. When Luke eventually climbed into his X-wing starfighter to attack the first Death Star at the Battle of Yavin, we rooted for Luke's victory because we cared about him.

Over the course of the three films, most of the principal characters evolved. Luke Skywalker changed from a wide-eyed farm boy to a Jedi Knight. Intergalactic smugglers Han Solo and Chewbacca and professional gambler Lando Calrissian became heroes of the Rebel Alliance. Princess Leia Organa realized that, yes, she really was in love with that scoundrel Solo. The droids C-3PO and R2-D2 developed a stronger friendship. Perhaps most significantly, Darth Vader learned he had not been entirely consumed by the dark side of the Force, and was still capable of selfless courage. Grand Moff Tarkin, Jabba the Hutt, and Emperor Palpatine were unwilling or unable to improve themselves . . . and were doomed.

This book features concise descriptions of many favorite *Star Wars* characters, plus a few who were only briefly glimpsed loitering on the streets of Mos Eisley or performing for Jabba the Hutt. On screen, these background aliens and droids stood out by their elaborate costumes and exotic appearances, but little was revealed of their personalities or unique quirks. As chronicled in the numerous *Star Wars* novels, short stories, and comic books, these characters appearing briefly in the film have extensively rich backgrounds of their own.

So if you thought all the aliens in the Mos Eisley cantina were villains and that Boba Fett died in the Sarlacc pit, brace yourself. The story is far from over!

Born on the watery world Mon Calamari, **Admiral Ackbar** was the leader of Coral City when Imperial forces invaded his world. After being rescued by the Rebel Alliance, Ackbar commanded his own personal flagship in the Alliance's surprise attack on the second Death Star.

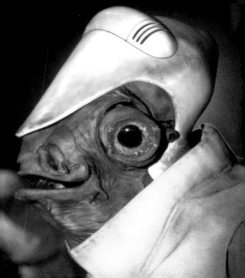

Barquin D'an

Although regarded as a less talented musician than his younger brother, bandleader of Figrin D'an and the Modal Nodes, **Barquin D'an** was an excellent songwriter. More than anything, Barquin hoped to find a steady gig off the desert planet Tatooine.

Luke Skywalker's foster mother had hoped to protect the young man from the secret truth about his father, but she knew his longing for adventure would take him away from Tatooine. The death of **Aunt Beru** and Uncle Owen at the hands of Imperial stormtroopers motivated Luke to follow Obi-Wan Kenobi on his voyage to Alderaan.

The Twi'lek **Bib Fortuna** was a slaver of his own people before he became Jabba the Hutt's chief lieutenant. Fortuna planned to kill the Hutt and take over his business, but the Twi'lek's efforts were thwarted by the arrival of a Rebel strikeforce led by Luke Skywalker at Jabba's palace on Tatooine.

On Tatooine, **Biggs Darklighter** was
Luke Skywalker's friend and role model.
After leaving the Imperial Space Academy,
Biggs told Luke of his plans to join the
Rebellion. The friends briefly reunited
on Yavin Four before piloting their
X-wings in the assault on the first Death
Star, during which Biggs was killed.

BOBA FETT

The most-feared bounty hunter in the galaxy, **Boba Fett** delivered Han Solo to Darth Vader and Jabba the Hutt, but was unprepared for Solo's escape from Tatooine. Despite initial reports of his demise, Boba Fett survived the Sarlacc creature and his nefarious work continued.

The Trandoshan **Bossk** was one of the bounty hunters who pursued Han Solo, hoping to gain the rewards offered by both Darth Vader and Jabba the Hutt. Like most Trandoshans, Bossk hated Wookiees and relished the chance to kill Solo's first mate, Chewbacca.

A golden protocol droid, **C-3PO** was fluent in over six million galactic languages. Although most droids routinely underwent memory wipes, C-3PO and his counterpart, R2-D2, had luckily retained most of their memories, making them a valuable asset to the Rebel Alliance.

As first officer on Darth Vader's *Executor*, **Captain Piett** assisted Admiral Ozzel in directing the fleet assigned to Vader's flagship. After Admiral Ozzel made a fatal mistake during the Imperial assault on the Rebel Base on Hoth, Piett was promoted to Admiral.

Chewbacca

Born on the tree-filled planet Kashyyyk, the more than two-centuries-old Wookiee **Chewbacca** is copilot of the *Millennium Falcon* and a loyal friend to Han Solo, the Corellian who rescued the Wookiee from an Imperial labor camp. The pair worked as smugglers before joining the Rebel Alliance.

DARTH
VADER

Born Anakin Skywalker, he became a
Jedi Knight and disciple of Obi-Wan
Kenobi. When he betrayed Kenobi to join
Palpatine in his bid for intergalactic
domination, he became **Darth Vader,**
Dark Lord of the Sith. Many years after
Vader helped the Emperor achieve this
end, his evil beliefs were challenged
by the son he never knew, a young Jedi
named Luke Skywalker.

Assigned the number 1023, **Davin Felth** was the stormtrooper who located a piece of an R2 unit near an escape pod on Tatooine. Mortified by the execution of Owen and Beru Lars by his commanding officer, Davin changed his allegiance and became a spy for the Rebel Alliance.

Dengar

Once a successful swoop jockey, **Dengar** was injured when he lost a race against Han Solo. Tossed out of the professional swoop circuit, Dengar became a freelance assassin who joined the bounty hunters hired by Darth Vader to hunt for Han Solo.

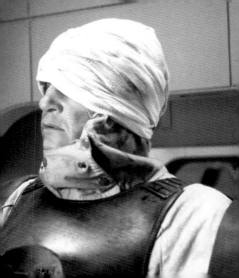

Dr. Evazan

An insane medical practioner, **Dr. Evazan** enjoyed what he called "creative surgery." Evazan had left a ghastly trail of victims and bore a horrible scar from a bounty hunter's blaster shot. Evazan boasted of having been sentenced to death in twelve star systems.

Growing up far from the planet Rodia, **Doda Bodonawieedo**'s parents fled to Tatooine to be free of Rodian tyranny. Doda learned how to play many instruments from his father and enjoyed performing with the Max Rebo Band.

DODA BODONAWIEEDO

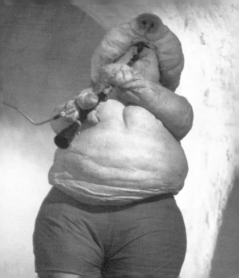

A Kitonak from Kirdo III, **Snit "Droopy" McCool** played a variety of wind instruments. Although he was a talented jizz wailer, Droopy longed to play the Kitonak love songs he remembered from his youth. Jabba's offer of free food hardly impressed Droopy, who had enough crated slugs to last for years.

McCool

Under the direction of Lord Darth Vader,
General Veers commanded the Imperial
ground troops for Vader's special armada.
When Vader learned of the secret Rebel
base on the ice planet Hoth, General
Veers personally supervised the invasion
force from his AT-AT walker.

8D8

A subordinate of EV-9D9, the thin-faced droid **8D8** worked in Jabba the Hutt's droid operations center. Like all the other droids in Jabba's palace, 8D8 lived in fear of EV-9D9, knowing that any mistake could lead to termination.

Emperor Palpatine

A former Senator for the Old Republic, **Palpatine** used political manipulation and the dark side of the Force to forge his Empire. He seduced Darth Vader to the dark side, and with his help initiated a vast military buildup as he crushed the remnants of the Old Republic.

A pachydermoid from the planet Vinsoth, **Ephant Mon** was the closest thing Jabba the Hutt had to a friend. They worked together as gunrunners until Jabba appointed Ephant as his secret internal security official, in charge of rooting out thievery and assassination plots.

A thin droid with a female voice, **EV-9D9** seemed to take sadistic delight in her job as Supervisor of droid operations for Jabba the Hutt. Believing it was her duty to work other droids until they dropped, EV-9D9 tortured or mutilated her numerous charges.

Leader of **Figrin D'an** and the Modal Nodes, this Bith bandleader and Kloo hornist played in nearly every lounge club in the galaxy. His band's brand of jizz music proved especially popular at the Mos Eisley cantina, where they were offered a two-season engagement.

4-LOM

Once a protocol droid, **4-LOM**'s programming was altered, transforming him into a master thief. Jabba the Hutt further expanded 4-LOM's programming, allowing the droid to respond to violence with deadly precision. 4-LOM was paired with Zuckuss in the bounty hunters' hunt for Han Solo.

Manufactured by Med-Tech, **FX-7** was an antique medical droid, specializing in the diagnosis and treatment of injury and disease. Serving the Rebels, the multiarmed FX-7 assisted 2-1B in the emergency medical facility on Hoth.

GARINDAN

Born on the arid planet Kubindi, **Garindan** the Kubaz operated as a spy on Tatooine. He was working for the Imperials when he trailed R2-D2 and C-3PO though Mos Eisley Spaceport. Later, Garindan led the stormtroopers to Docking Bay 94 and the *Millennium Falcon*.

Once a highly-decorated Imperial officer, **General Crix Madine** defected to the Rebel Alliance. At the Battle of Endor, Madine helped devise the plan for a small strike team to deactivate the incomplete Death Star's shield so the battle station could be attacked.

A retired officer for the Old Republic, **General Dodonna** was considered too old to be retrained for the Empire. Targeted for assassination by Imperials, he joined the Rebel Alliance. A brilliant strategist, Dodonna coordinated the assault on the first Death Star.

One of the Emperor's most loyal administrators, **Grand Moff Tarkin** was an Imperial governor with an unquenchable thirst for power. Tarkin conceived and was the architect of the first Death Star, the ultimate realization of the Emperor's doctrine to rule by fear.

The Rodian beauty **Greeata** was skilled at playing the Kloo horn as well as using it as a weapon. Greeata's longtime friend Sy Snootles refused Max Rebo's offer to join his band unless he also hired Greeata. Rebo hired them both on the spot.

The foul-smelling Rodian named **Greedo** wanted nothing more than to be a bounty hunter. Hoping to impress Jabba the Hutt, Greedo attempted to capture Han Solo on his own in the Mos Eisley Cantina. Despite having the drop on Solo, the Rodian was no match for the Corellian smuggler.

HanSolo

The Corellian captain of the *Millennium Falcon* got away with his large ego because he was quick with a blaster and a great starpilot. A former intergalactic smuggler, **Han Solo** surprised many when he and his copilot Chewbacca enlisted with the Rebellion.

A Jawa from Tatooine, **Jek Nkik** was a skilled mechanic. His clan sold a scavenged protocol droid and an R2 unit to a moisture farmer. Unfortunately, the two droids were later sought by Imperial stormtroopers who then destroyed Jek Nkik's sandcrawler.

JEK
NKIK

Designed as an assassin droid at Holowan Laboratories, **IG-88** immediately asserted his independence by murdering his programmers. Although forty systems wanted IG-88 "dismantled on sight," the droid was summoned by Darth Vader to join in the hunt for Han Solo.

A gangster who ran his great criminal empire from the desert planet Tatooine, **Jabba the Hutt** was enraged when smuggler Han Solo dumped a shipment of glitterstim spice to avoid Imperial entanglements. Holding Solo responsible for the lost fortune, Jabba placed an enormous bounty on Solo's head. Solo's capture proved Jabba's undoing when the smuggler's friends clashed with him at the Sarlacc pit, where Jabba was strangled by Princess Leia.

A Yuzzum from the planet Howda, **Joh Yowza** was traveling with a religious troupe when he fell under the spell of jizz-wailer music. Much to his elder's consternation, Yowza quit his troupe and joined the Max Rebo Band.

Soldier-of-fortune **Lando Calrissian** owned the *Millennium Falcon* before losing the ship to Han Solo in a game of sabacc. Before joining the Rebellion, Lando was Baron Administrator of Bespin's Cloud City where he betrayed Han Solo in the hopes of appeasing the Empire. When Darth Vader double-crossed him, he led an insurrection and joined in rescuing Solo from Jabba the Hutt. Later, he led the Rebel assault on the second Death Star.

The cyborg named **Lobot** was Lando Calrissian's administrative aid on Bespin's Cloud City. A brain-enhancing device allowed Lobot to remain in constant contact with the city's central computers. Following Calrissian's signal, Lobot aided the Rebels against the invading stormtroopers.

LOBOT

Raised on the desert planet Tatooine, **Luke Skywalker** yearned for adventure in space. Soon after Obi-Wan Kenobi introduced Luke to the ways of the Force, Luke joined the Rebellion against the Empire and began his training as a Jedi Knight under Yoda. Ultimately, he confronted Darth Vader and the Emperor himself during the Rebel assault on the second Death Star.

Luke
Skywalker

The Ortolan leader of the **Max Rebo** Band played keyboards on his Red Ball Jett organ. When the jizz-wailer band came to the attention of Jabba the Hutt, Max Rebo was offered a lifetime contract for all the food he could eat. An ever-hungry fellow, Rebo couldn't refuse, and his band became a fixture at Jabba's court.

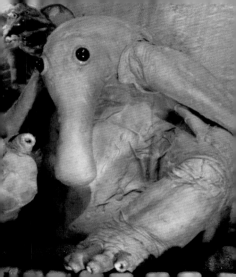

After **Momaw Nadon** was forced to betray his peaceful species' agricultural secrets to the Empire, he was banished from his homeworld Ithor. On Tatooine, the exiled Ithorian—also known as Hammerhead—worked with the Rebel underground, aiding the Alliance in any way he could.

MON MOTHMA

Before Palpatine declared himself Emperor, **Mon Mothma** had been the senior Senator of the Old Republic. Under threat from Imperial assassination squads, she went underground to form the Alliance to Restore the Republic. Her efforts inspired many systems to join what became known as the Rebel Alliance.

A native of the planet Sullust, **Nien Nunb** was a trade runner for a mineral-processing company until his employers sided with the Empire. He joined the Rebellion, and was chosen by Lando Calrissian to copilot the *Millennium Falcon* in the Battle of Endor.

Believed by many to be a mere hermit on Tatooine, old Ben Kenobi was in fact **Obi-Wan Kenobi**, a heroic Jedi Knight who had served in the Clone Wars. Summoned by Princess Leia to join the Rebel Alliance, Obi-Wan Kenobi introduced Luke Skywalker to the ways of the Force and was killed by his former pupil Darth Vader on the first Death Star.

Oola

Kidnapped from the planet Ryloth by her fellow Twi'lek Bib Fortuna, **Oola** was delivered as a slave for Jabba the Hutt. In Jabba's court, Oola performed as a dancer, entertaining the Hutt and doing her best to avoid his advances.

Owen Lars

Luke Skywalker's foster father was a moisture farmer on Tatooine. Because he knew more about Luke's family history than he revealed, **Owen Lars** did his best to discourage Luke from leaving the desert planet and enrolling in the Imperial Space Academy.

An Aqualish from the planet Ando, **Pondo Baba** was an intergalactic pirate and murderer. Baba lost an arm to Obi-Wan Kenobi's lightsaber after Baba and his partner, Dr. Evazan, assaulted Luke Skywalker in the Mos Eisley Cantina.

Raised on Alderaan, **Princess Leia** fought for reforms in the Imperial Senate before she joined the Alliance to Restore the Republic. Leia's effort to locate and recruit Obi-Wan Kenobi led to her famous rescue by Luke Skywalker and Han Solo.

The astromech utility droid **R2-D2** was bolder than his cautious friend, C-3PO. Despite his apparently limited vocabulary of beeps and whistles, he was a skilled mechanic, and was also able to interface with ship computers. He navigated Luke Skywalker's X-wing during the attack on the first Death Star, and on subsequent flights.

Owen Lars didn't need a navigator but a good mechanic when he bought **R5-D4** from the Jawas. Unknown to Lars or the Jawas, R5-D4 had allowed R2-D2 to program his motivator to blow up. R5-D4's "malfunction" was a sacrifice that allowed R2-D2 and C-3PO to stay together.

Born Rapotwanatantonee, the Shawda Ubb of Manpha changed his name to **Rappertunie** and joined the Max Rebo Band. Admired for his talent with an electonically enhanced growdi, Rappertunie was careful not to become food in Jabba's court.

The three-eyed Gran from the planet Kinyen, **Ree-Yees** was obnoxious and antagonistic. No one knew how the unpleasant creature wormed his way into Jabba's palace, but it was suspected that Jabba enjoyed seeing Ree-Yees start fights with Ephant Mon because Ephant always won.

Rystáll

An exotic halfbreed from Coruscant, **Rystáll** was abandoned by her mother and raised by Ortolan musicians. She grew to be a talented singer and dancer. Rystáll's adoptive parents were old friends of Droopy McCool, who invited her to tour with Max Rebo.

The cackling Kowakian monkey lizard
Salacious Crumb greatly amused Jabba
the Hutt, who hired Crumb to make him
laugh. Crumb kept close to Jabba, feed-
ing off whatever food fell from the Hutt's
mouth and taking care not to wind up
as an accidental snack.

The occasional lead singer for the Max Rebo Band was known for her incredible stage presence as well as her dynamic voice. Besides free food, **Sy Snootles** earned quite a bit of money as a court spy for Bib Fortuna.

SNOOTLES

After the Imperial invasion of his home-world of Mon Calamari, the Quarren named **Tessek** fled to Tatooine and became an accountant for Jabba the Hutt. For years, Tessek embezzeled Jabba's money, hoping to one day escape Jabba and set up business for himself. His plans were foiled as a result of the Rebel strikeforce's daring rescue of Han Solo.

An older medical droid in service for
the Rebel Alliance, **2-1B** was a skilled
surgeon and field medic. On Hoth, 2-1B
treated Luke Skywalker's injuries from
an encounter with a wampa ice creature.
The droid operated on him again after
the young Jedi's lightsaber battle with
Darth Vader on Cloud City.

The Corellian-born **Wedge Antilles** was an ace X-wing starfighter pilot and commander of Rogue Squadron. Wedge fought the Empire in the Battles of Yavin, Hoth, and Endor, and had the distinction of being the only Rebel pilot to attack both Death Stars.

The Ewok named **Wicket W. Warrick** found Princess Leia Organa after her speeder bike chase on the forest moon of Endor. A brave warrior, Wicket convinced the rest of his tribe to aid the Rebels in disabling the Imperial shield generator for the second Death Star.

Yoda

For more than eight hundred years, the diminutive Jedi Master trained students in the ways of the Force. After the Emperor ordered his purge of the Jedi Knights, **Yoda** went into hiding on the swamp planet Dagobah. Two of Yoda's best students were Obi-Wan Kenobi and Luke Skywalker.